I0439742

REXY

The Hill of Courage

Written by: **Sharon Bloch**

Illustrated by: **Murriam Saeed**

Copyright © 2016 by Sharon Bloch

Rexy is a sweet, friendly Dalmatian.
When he is happy, he wiggles his tail
and a big puppy smile appears on
his face. Rexy has a black spot on his back,
shaped like a heart and his mommy
says that he is a puppy of love.

Rexy's summer vacation was filled with adventures. He spent time at the beach, surfed, went on excursions, ate ice cream, and watched all the puppy movies that were shown at the movie theater.
And now, just as he ran out of ideas for new ways to have fun, and he started to get a little bit bored, the new school year was about to begin.

Rexy was happy to go back to school and see his class-mates, and he was even happier to go back because he was going to join the school's soccer team. He practiced a lot so he would make the team and fulfill his dream: to stand at the goal post with the blue goal-keeper's uniform, and block all the balls.

In the morning, Mommy woke him up. She was holding a letter from the soccer team's coach. Rexy sat on his bed, barked enthusiastically, and read the letter out loud. Mommy looked at him; she was excited as well. "My puppy is already big, and now he is going to be the goalie of the soccer team," she said.

"Tomorrow morning the Owls will babysit your little sister and we will go buy you everything you need for the team, as well as a new soccer ball."

The next day, Rexy woke up very early. Everyone was still asleep and he couldn't help himself, he woke his mom up. "Mommy, wake up. Let's go already!"He said, shaking her lightly. Rexy's mommy opened her eyes, smiled and got out of bed. They ate their breakfast and when the Owls came to babysit Pitsy, they headed out.

Rexy was ecstatic! Pitsy had stayed home, Mommy was all his, and this shopping day was all for him. They went into the big sports store. There was fitness equipment ,weights, uniforms for different soccer teams, and balls of all types.

Rexy ran around enthusiastically and wiggled his tail. "Woof! Woof! Look at this blue ball!" He said to Mommy. "And wait; look at this red uniform, and these large weights. Woof! Woof! Please buy them for me!"

"Slow down Rexy," Mommy answered. "Let's look on the list and you can choose what you want and need."

Rexy took the list from his pocket and took everything he needed off the shelves.

White socks – check! Goalie's gloves – check! Knee pads – check! Soccer shoes – check! Blue goalie's uniform – check! And the most important thing – soccer ball – check!

Once he collected everything from the list, he was very excited. His tongue flopped out of his mouth, he hyperventilated, and a huge smile spread across his face. "I am a big puppy! I will be an excellent goalie!" Rexy barked out loud.

Mommy picked a big bag for Rexy and put all the equipment inside it. After she paid the saleswoman for the equipment, she called for Rexy to help her carry it all to the car. The bag was heavy and Rexy helped her, but he complained about it.

"I am very proud of you, Rexy," Mommy said as they began driving. "I am sure you will put a lot of effort into soccer, and you will be an excellent goalie."

"And what if I don't?" Rexy asked.

Rexy's mommy heard a lot of fear in her puppy's voice.

"Sweetie, what's worrying you?" she asked.

There was silence in the car, and Rexy, who up until a moment ago was happy and excited, became more and more nervous and serious.

Mommy tried again. "What happened to your mood?"

Rexy didn't answer, and they drove the rest of the way home without speaking.

After exiting the car Mommy told Rexy, "I see that something is bothering you. I'm going to make lunch now, and I want you to know that I would be happy if you would share it with me."

Rexy went to his room. He sat on his bed, looked at all his new things and although he really wanted to, he couldn't be happy.

Mean while, Mommy cooked lunch and waited patiently. She really wanted to go into Rexy's room, but she knew that he needed time to understand and to feel.

Once she was finished cooking, she dried her paws and went to see how her puppy was doing.

She knocked on the door of his room and asked, "Are you ready to share with me?"

"Yes," Rexy replied. Mommy entered the room and sat by his side.

"Mommy, what will happen if I don't succeed?
What will happen if I don't block the goals at the post?
What will happen if all my friends on the team make
fun of me and say that I am a bad goalie?"

Mommy hugged Rexy tightly and said, "My darling
puppy, I understand that you are worried,
it's natural. Let's talk about your fear. Let's get
to know it together."

Rexy hugged Mommy tightly and cried. Mommy let him get all the fear out, because she knew that in her arms he felt safe. Slowly, he calmed down. Rexy looked into Mommy's eyes and told her, "I'm scared! I fear I will not be a good goalie! I don't want to join the soccer team anymore, and I don't want to be a goalie at all!"

"My Rexy," Mommy said, and looked at him with loving eyes. "You say you don't want to join the soccer team and you don't want to be a goalie. I know you are scared, it is scary to try something new, but do you really not want to be a goalie on the team?"

Rexy thought for several minutes, and then said, "It's not that I don't want to, it's just that I am afraid that I won't be any good at it."

"Let's close our eyes and imagine something together, okay?" Mommy said.

"Okay," Rexy replied.

"Imagine we are standing at the goal-post on the soccer field. What do you feel?"

"I'm scared."

"Good. You are allowed to be scared," Mommy said.
"I am with you .Feel it. Let's get closer to it and get to
know it. What color is it in your imagination?"

Rexy thought for a second and said, "It is a gray color."

"What do you feel in your body when you are scared?"

"Like I am standing in cold, wet ,mud."

"Come Rexy; let's stand together inside the mud.
Can you feel it?"

"Yes. My feet feel cold."

"What are you thinking about right now when you stand here in the mud?"

"I don't think I will succeed. Balls will come my way and I will not be able to stop them! I think that everybody will laugh at me and that the coach will be angry at me!"

"And how do you feel now?"

"I feel bad and I feel sad." Rexy felt tears suffocate his throat.

"So now," Mommy told Rexy, "it is time to get out of the mud and look at your fear from a different, higher place. This place is called the hill of courage, and it's really close by. Can you see the hill? What color is it?"

"It's green, filled with grass."

"Can you climb up it? It's not easy."

"Yes, I can. It is not difficult at all, Mommy."

"Way to go my puppy. Keep climbing."

Rexy kept climbing in his imagination until he reached the top of the hill of courage.

"I did it mommy!" Rexy barked, excitedly.

"And how do you feel now?"

"I feel good, a little bit like how I feel when I chase cats in the neighborhood and the wind is blowing on my fur," Rexy replied and a little smile spread across his face.

"Now that you are up here, look at the mud that you were in earlier. Can you see it down there?"

"Yes Mommy, I can see it. It is far away from me and I don't want to be there again."

"In that case, you can open your eyes," Mommy said.

Rexy opened his eyes, took a deep breath, and said, "Mommy, I do want to be the goalie on the soccer team. I am fast and I jump high and I am going to block all those balls!"

"So where did you like it more – in the mud or on the hill of courage?"

Rexy did not hesitate. "It's the best up on the green hill of courage!"

Mommy was proud of him and hugged him tightly. Together they went to have lunch.

Mommy explained to Rexy that with the help of your imagination you can choose where you want to be.

"Remember this, my puppy," Mommy said. "The hill of courage will always be there, even when you don't close your eyes."

Rexy listened to Mommy and ate with delight. When he was done, he ran to his room and tried on his new goalie uniform.

Dear sweet KIDS

My name is Sharon. It is so nice to meet you!

For many years I was a Kindergarten teacher and loved to read books to the kids in my class.

I used to make up stories to help them when they were upset, and teach them how to be happy and positive about themselves and about their life.

Rexy was born in my heart during those years, and I made up many stories about him, that the kids loved!

In our daily life we feel fear many times. Sometimes we are so afraid it makes us stop doing things or even avoid them.

Fear is part of our life and we should learn to come closer and to get a nd know our fear and change what we think so we can feel better.

 "Rexy The Hill Of Courge" present a way to change our thoughts and feelings when we are afraid of change. This way we can make our daily life better and happier.

I believe that it is very important for children to grow up knowing that they can create and affect their reality by choosing a positive way to get closer to their fears.

It is my dream and big wish that you will know Rexy, Love Rexy and learn with Rexy how to have a positive attitude and understanding that we can make our life happier by choosing a positive way of dealing with fears..

I wish and hope that Rexy will touch your heart just like he touched mine.

Thank you so much! Big hugs!

DEAR PARENTS

Rexy is just like your child. What Rexy goes through, happens to him/her as well.

Using Rexy's story, I invite you to get a better understanding of your child and I offer ways to help him.

For a long time Rexy has dreamt of the moment he would get to join the soccer team, and now that his dream is about to come true, he is filled with fear. He stands before a big challenge that forces him to get out of his comfort zone, break his routine and try something new.

Rexy is afraid of the future and the unknown. He is afraid of change.

Changes occur all the time in all of our lives. Our body changes, our thoughts change, nature and environment change, our plans change, our needs change…

Everything changes all the time, and yet, we are all afraid of changes.

In order to face our fears, we hang on to our routine, and to what is known to us, and to those who give us security. The need to feel secure is bigger in children, and that is why they love routine. They are not bored by it, they are calmed by it, and it makes them feel like they are in control. They like to hear the same story again and again, to watch the same movie, and to walk down the same road.

Routine is not a bad thing, but changes are inevitable, they are needed in order to develop and advance in life and we must know how to deal with them.

This is a daily conflict and we must know how to balance the two poles – routine and change.

Our mind doesn't like surprises, especially bad ones. That is why it prepares us for the worst. Every bad scenario goes in our child's mind before a change occurs, just so that he isn't caught unprepared. That is how the mind works. That is its defense mechanism.

These scenarios and the accompanying worry are very tiring and they empty all of our child's inner strength. In addition to that, he thinks that he is a coward – which makes the combination twice as bad.

That is why it is important to give our children a place to feel their worries and fears. We must explain to him that fear is a natural, positive emotion and it exists in all of us.

If we try to run away from the fear, or ignore it, it becomes stronger. That is why we need to let it be, to look at it, to understand, feel it, and talk about it.

For many years I have used my imagination to deal with my own fear of challenging changes and I use it in my work with children.

Children go into the imaginary world easily. Everyone experiences fear differently, in a different color, different feelings and thoughts, but each child can climb upon his own hill of courage. When he is at the top he can look from another point of view at the place where he was before. The ability to look from another point of view helps our child to get out of himself and come back again with a better understanding of himself feeling connected to his inner strengths.

We parents need to learn not to panic over our child's fears. He needs us to contain the fear and get to know it and not annul it. Annulling achieves the opposite result and our child remains alone with a fear he thinks he is not allowed to feel. With the help of guiding questions, we can connect our child with his fear, teach him how to feel it, accept it as a natural and allowed thing, and from there we can help him to find the strength to get over it.

Guiding Questions

Imagine you are physically in a new place that wakes your fear (the soccer field, at the dentist's office, in a new school, when you come home with the new baby, etc.)

Where in your body do you feel the fear?

What color does the fear have?

What shape does the fear have?

What feeling does the fear have? Is it hot? Is it cold? Is it wet? Smooth? Rough?

The idea is to create a solid image, something familiar and therefore closer.

Once you have this image, you may go on and ask about the thought:

When you feel the fear, what are you thinking? What can happen? What do you imagine?

And the next step is – What do you feel? What feeling does it make in your heart? Does it feel good?

Now comes the most important part, and that is the connection with the inner strength and our child's faith in himself.

Take him, in his imagination, to a high place, the hill of courage, and there repeat the process. Enforce and strengthen the positive feelings and remind your child how much stronger he feels and how capable he is of dealing with his fear.

I invite you to get to know the fear and climb up on top of your own hill of courage.

GOOD LUCK!

Love,

Sharon Bloch